ONE VOTE

#1 *NEW YORK TIMES* BESTSELLING AUTHOR

BEN CARSON, MD

WITH CANDY CARSON

MAKE YOUR VOICE HEARD

Tyndale House Publishers, Inc.
Carol Stream, Illinois

Visit Tyndale online at www.tyndale.com.

TYNDALE and Tyndale's quill logo are registered trademarks of Tyndale House Publishers, Inc.

One Vote: Make Your Voice Heard

Designed by Jacqueline L. Nuñez

Cover design by Kristin Arbuckle

Published in association with Yates & Yates (www.yates2.com).

For discounts on bulk orders of this book, please contact:
Tyndale House Publishers
351 S. Executive Drive
Carol Stream, Illinois 60188
1-855-277-9400

Any Internet addresses (websites, blogs, etc.) in this book are offered as a resource. They are not intended in any way to be or imply an endorsement by the author or any parties associated with the publication of the book of the content of these sites for the life of this book.

ISBN 978-1-4964-0632-3

Printed in the United States of America

20	19	18	17	16	15	14
7	6	5	4	3	2	1

*This book is dedicated to the many
Americans who sacrificed so that we all can
now have the privilege of one vote.*

CONTENTS

ACKNOWLEDGMENTS

OUR DEEP APPRECIATION goes to Sealy Yates, Craig Michaelis, and Mick Yates for their hard work in bringing this project together.

PREFACE

SEVERAL YEARS AGO, after the usual arduous twelve-to-sixteen-hour day at work as the director of pediatric neurosurgery at Johns Hopkins Hospital, I was rushing home to complete my civic duty as a voter in Maryland's gubernatorial race. I lived in Upperco, Maryland, and my polling place was right down the street at a fire station. I arrived five minutes before 8 p.m., which was the closing time for the polls. After waiting in line for a few minutes, I was told the polls were closed and those still waiting in line would not be permitted to vote. I was considerably less than amused and felt deprived of a constitutional right.

It was one of the few times I have missed a voting opportunity since I reached the age of majority while in college. I remember being very excited about my first opportunity to vote for a presidential candidate while a student at Yale. Like most of the students there at that time, I considered myself a liberal and proudly voted for George McGovern, who lost in a landslide. My political leanings have changed significantly over the years based on my experiences. Although I probably lean more toward the conservative side now, my interest in participating in the selection of our representatives has not diminished. In fact, now that I have children and grandchildren, I have even more interest in trying to protect their future with my *one vote*.

Recent polling has shown that the vast majority of Americans feel our nation is moving in the wrong direction, and many people feel powerless to do anything about it. This is why *we the people* must undergo a radical change in our perception of who we are and how much power we have. We are at the pinnacle of power because our system of governance was set up that way.

There are few things in our lives that compare to the privilege and the responsibility we have as voters. Many people feel that their *one vote* does not count because they are only one among millions, but the sad fact is that in the 2012 presidential election, 93 million eligible voters failed to vote,[1] many of them feeling that their vote simply did not matter. Even a small fraction of that number of votes could dramatically affect the outcome of any election.

In the early days of America's history, only the rich and privileged were allowed to vote. Everyone else's right to vote was won after a hard-fought battle and should not be so easily relinquished. Voting is the only way we can control our government. If we fail to exercise that right, we are in danger of abdicating to our government the one power we all have in common—our *one vote*. What a terrible thing to believe that our *one vote* does not matter. It most certainly does. The next couple of national elections in America will determine what kind of country the future will hold. Each of us who plans on living here should certainly make sure, through our voting, that it is the place where we truly want to live.

After my unpleasant experience at the fire station in Upperco, Maryland, I began voting by absentee ballot and never had another anxious moment due to my unpredictable schedule. As the reader will learn in this publication, there are many avenues we can pursue to take advantage of our voting rights without creating undue turmoil in our lives.

CHAPTER 1

YOU ARE THE PINNACLE OF POWER

All power is originally vested in, and consequently derived from, the people. That government is instituted and ought to be exercised for the benefit of the people; which consists in the enjoyment of life and liberty, with the right of acquiring property, and generally of pursuing and obtaining happiness and safety. That the people have an indubitable, inalienable, and indefeasible right to reform or change their Government, whenever it may be found adverse or inadequate to the purposes of its institution.

JAMES MADISON

THE STATEMENT ON THE PRECEDING PAGE by our fourth president, often hailed as the "Father of the Constitution," makes it very clear that our founders intended for America to be governed by the will of the people. Too many previously well-intentioned governments had degenerated into monarchies or tyrannical states.

By vesting the power of the vote in the people themselves, the Founding Fathers fervently hoped and prayed the people would remain vigilant enough to recognize when (through their natural tendencies) elected officials began to overstep their boundaries and impose their will on the people. They expected that each man's *one vote* would be used to peacefully remove those who didn't deserve their elected offices.

The founders knew that prosperity would bring complacency and pave the way for the gradual erosion of a people-centric government. Our Constitution was designed to give people the option of taking corrective action without the need for the armed combat that too often happens around the world, even in this century. Our founders did, however, recognize there was a possibility that an overbearing government, drunk with power, might not submit to the will of the people and might, in fact, employ the military to suppress the will of the people. This is one of the reasons why the Second Amendment was added. It reads as follows: "A well-regulated militia, being necessary to the security of a free State, the right of the people to keep and bear arms, shall not be infringed." They knew that an armed populace would be a powerful deterrent to the imposition of dictatorial powers. As a testimony to their wisdom, a historical analysis informs us that many dictators, such as Hitler, Stalin, Castro, and Chairman Mao, among others, confiscated firearms before their reigns of terror began.

Through the power of the ballot, if *we the people* become unhappy with the direction of our government, we have the ability to make small changes or, through major gains in elections, even massive changes to the balance of power. Unfortunately, in recent years many people who are unhappy with the direction of the country have simply decided to tune out and let everyone else make the decisions. As I mentioned earlier, most people are unaware that in the presidential election of 2012, more people did not vote than voted for either candidate.

Having had an opportunity to meet with many of these disaffected voters, I have learned that large numbers of Americans have simply given up on the concept of a country of, by, and for the people and have decided that the downward spiral of our nation cannot be countered. Thus, they have given up.

This is just the kind of attitude that our founders wished to avoid by placing the real power in the hands of the people. This power gives the people the ability to meet with one another, discuss the direction of their nation, and, through their collective determination and voting, to change that direction. This is a wonderful blessing for every American, regardless of political affiliation.

Our system was designed to prevent anyone in any position from escaping the will of the people. Even the president, vice president, and Supreme Court justices (who hold lifetime positions) can be impeached through established parliamentary procedures if they have committed high crimes or treasonous acts. There are few places in the world that provide the people with so much power, and we must not only learn how to use it but understand our responsibility to use it correctly. Furthermore, we must vigilantly guard our rights as voters. There is no question that from time to time the people will be led astray by disingenuous politicians who are more interested in their party or their ideology than they are in the welfare of the nation. Knowing this to be the case, Thomas Jefferson famously said, "The good sense of the people will always be found to be the best army. They may be led astray for a moment, but will soon correct themselves."[1]

How do *we the people* know when the government is overstepping its boundaries and infringing on our rights? The first step in this realization is to understand that the government works for us and not vice versa. Whenever we see governmental policies that impose laws and regulations the majority of people oppose, we should question whether it is time to replace the leaders who would advocate for such a situation. Furthermore, when any of our basic rights—such as freedom of expression, freedom of religion, the right to our earned property, and so on—are compromised by executive decree or legislative processes, the alarm must be sounded, and we must rigorously resist the imposition of such measures on our lives. Heavy-handed tactics that are coercive and oppositional to the will of the people should not and cannot be tolerated, or they will only get worse and freedom will not be maintained. It is easy to fall into the trap of only acknowledging government overreaches when the party to which we do not belong is in charge. This is one of the reasons why Jesus once said (and Abraham Lincoln famously quoted), "A house divided against itself cannot stand."[2] When we can only recognize wrongdoing in a party other than our own, we are putting politics ahead of patriotism. When the majority of people are doing that, the viability of the nation is threatened.

I mentioned earlier that some people have simply tuned out of the political process and have refused to participate because they are discouraged. There are others, however, who have developed attitudes more characteristic of spoiled children who, upon failing to get their way, simply say, "I'm taking my marbles and going home." This is different from those who simply tune out of the game of marbles in the first place. These people need to realize that in the world of representative government, which is what we have, it is actually smart to use your resources to pick the lesser of two evils. It is fallacious reasoning to conclude that all people who are not your chosen candidate are equally bad. No one who fails to vote has any right to complain about the government that is put in place.

In the case that I mentioned in the preface, where I was denied the right to vote because I was tardy according to the election officials, the whole problem could have been avoided with some forethought. In order to avoid such situations, it is important to plan ahead as you would with any important event in your life. That might mean arranging for someone to watch your children, or even planning to take the children with you to the voting booth. Sometimes it involves making arrangements with an employer ahead of time. Also, everyone should be aware that most states allow you to vote by absentee ballot in any election so long as arrangements are made in advance. And it is important to note that in many cases you do not have to be away from home on election day to be eligible to vote by absentee ballot. It is helpful to know you can mail in your absentee ballot at any time after you receive it in the mail until the day of the election. The point is, performing your civic duty as a voter is considerably more important than watching your favorite television program or sporting event. Even though it doesn't cost you anything to vote, it could cost you a great deal of unhappiness not to.

I wish I did not have to include the next few sentences, but unfortunately, I must. There are many people who go to the polls and vote for people about whom they know very little. In many cases, they are only looking for the political designation and sometimes vote a straight Republican ticket or a straight Democrat ticket without paying any attention whatsoever to who these people are or what the issues are. If, in fact, they were to study some of the candidates they were voting for, they would be horrified. They would find that these people have little in common with them, and in many cases, they actually vote in ways contrary to the well-being of their constituency. Later in this book, we will discuss some of the mechanisms that can be easily employed by anyone to garner a great deal of information about candidates for public office.

It is very important for voters to beware of groups trying to buy their votes with material goods or special privileges. Voters should be particularly wary of those who only show up around election time, contributing nothing worthwhile throughout the remainder of the year. If these are good and decent people, those characteristics should be manifested 24/7, 365 days a year. When that is the case, it is very unlikely they will find it necessary to try to buy votes. It is also critical for all voters to use their analytical skills and not wait for someone else to tell them how they should vote. It is a simple matter to ask yourself whether the policies that various candidates are advocating have been helpful or harmful to you and your community. If the community is not improving and the same political figures have been around for quite some time, common sense would dictate the necessity for a change. Until they awaken, people who cannot make that simple calculation are destined to continue with their less-than-optimal lifestyles.

We have all been admonished to vote responsibly, but what does that really mean? I believe it simply means we should be familiar with the choices offered on the ballot and employ our cognitive skills to make choices in our best interests. Always voting for one party or as someone else instructed you shows you are not taking your responsibility as a voter seriously, and it also makes you the kind of voter candidates do not take seriously, because they conclude you are easily manipulated. If you want candidates to engage in responsibly courting your vote, you must demand they explain in an intelligible way what they have done to deserve it.

Many years ago, it was common for high schools to offer courses in civics. In these courses, students learned, among other things, about the structure of government and about their responsibilities as voters. Many, if not most, schools have now eliminated such courses, perhaps assuming this kind of material will be learned by osmosis. As part of that osmotic process, parents, guardians, and relatives should begin to explain civic responsibilities and the democratic process to young people as soon as they are able to comprehend them. If you look at some of the exit exams people had to take to get a certificate for completion of the eighth grade in the early to mid-1800s, you will see the students were expected to have a broad base of knowledge in civics. When students have this kind of information, they generally become much more interested in the local, national, and international news and are much more likely to become informed citizens.

Few privileges or responsibilities are more important than that of voting. *We the people* have the ability to control the destiny of our nation. We should never be in the position of giving up in despair. The founders of this nation put in place a structure to preserve life, liberty, and the pursuit of happiness. It is up to us to use it.

CHAPTER 2

KNOWLEDGE IS POWER

To make democracy work, we must be a nation of participants, not simply observers. One who does not vote has no right to complain.

LOUIS L'AMOUR

WHEN I WAS IN THE FIFTH GRADE, I was truly amazed by the depth of knowledge displayed by some of my classmates, while I knew virtually nothing that seemed to matter in the classroom. The same smart kids not only displayed impressive funds of knowledge about history, but were also comfortable talking about math, science, geography, music, and practically everything the teacher brought up. I secretly admired them but never imagined that I could compete with them intellectually. Much to my displeasure, my mother imposed a rather draconian reading program on me and my brother, Curtis, that completely reversed our lackluster academic performance. Within eighteen months, I went from the bottom of the class to the top of the class, and many of those smart kids were now asking me for the answers. Some have described this academic metamorphosis as miraculous, but in fact, it is the kind of transformation I have witnessed or heard about countless times when people fill their time with reading and the acquisition of knowledge as opposed to worthless pursuits of near-constant entertainment. I am not disparaging sports and entertainment, which certainly have their appropriate place in our lives, but that place should not be the pinnacle of our priorities.

Knowledge not only changed my perception of who I was, but it later had a profound impact on important decisions in my life. For example, even though I went to a mostly black high school in Detroit during the height of Motown's influence and I wanted desperately to be cool, I became interested in classical music and began playing the euphonium. I was even offered a prestigious music scholarship, although I turned it down at the suggestion of one of my teachers, who felt that I had a great medical career ahead of me and did not want me to get distracted.

Nevertheless, I continue to cultivate my interest in classical music, and it has resulted in many friendships that would otherwise have eluded me. As I reflect on ice-breaking conversations with colleagues and patients about music over the years, I realize that my knowledge of classical music may have opened doors for me in my medical career.

Most important, my musical interests led to

my involvement with a young Yale violinist who eventually became my wife. Our three sons became musicians and, along with my wife, formed a string quartet called the Carson Four, performing across the country before they disbanded as the kids grew up and went their separate ways. After nearly forty years of marriage, our musical passion remains one of our many mutual joys.

Obviously, my knowledge of classical music has had life-altering consequences for me. And the amount and the kinds of knowledge you acquire will play a huge role in directing the course of your life too. Do not worry about taxing your brain with too much information. As a neuroscientist, I can unequivocally assure you that it is impossible to overload the human brain with knowledge. Your brain retains everything you have ever seen or heard or experienced in any way and has plenty of capacity beyond that.

The more you know, the more doors will be open to you. When you stop and think about it, you must conclude that it is a wonderful thing to be able to increase your opportunities by your own efforts.

At first, it may seem to be a daunting, if not impossible, task to become a well-informed individual in this complex, information-driven world we live in. I certainly felt that way when I was called "dummy" in the fifth grade. My view, and everyone else's, of my capabilities dramatically changed as I became a bookworm, consuming multiple books every week with great relish.

This same kind of transition is possible for anyone with a normal brain, but it requires determination and consistency. At first, reading is not fun for someone who is hooked on electronic media and entertainment. However, the more one reads, the easier it becomes to comprehend the material and to activate the imagination.

When you watch television, you can certainly learn many things, but you are largely engaged in *passive* learning. (Whoever came up with the idea for the television program you are watching was undoubtedly the beneficiary of *active* learning.) The processes of active and passive learning have very different effects on your brain. When you read, you must transform sentences into mental concepts, requiring a great deal more brain activity than passive learning does. That is the reason why it is much easier to remember material that one reads rather than watches on a screen.

On the lecture circuit, I frequently challenge audiences the way my mother, who had only a third-grade education, challenged me and my brother (who went on to become an engineer). She made us read. I encourage you to read about something new for one half hour every day, seven days a week, 365 days per year. Thirty minutes is certainly not a great deal of time, considering that many people daily spend several hours watching television.

If you are willing to spend a half hour per day reading, you will be delightfully surprised by how your knowledge base and confidence level increase over the course of one year. I guarantee that people who have not seen you on a regular basis will be genuinely shocked by your increased ability to converse intelligently on a wide variety of subjects. You will be much better at communicating and defending your positions and will be much less likely to engage in name-calling and demonization of those with whom you disagree.

You can read about a variety of different topics, but make sure to include science, math, and technology, because we live in an increasingly sophisticated society, and many of the problems facing our country are related to finance, health, and energy. Many people will balk, saying, "I was never good in science or math, and such things do not interest me." Don't worry. You don't have to read textbooks to start. Popular publications abound. The magazine that put me on a path to neuroscience was *Psychology Today*, a subscription my brother gave me as a present when we were kids.

Science and math may seem too difficult to

learn, but in many ways they are like reading. If you know all twenty-six letters of the alphabet, you are on your way to reading. If you only know twenty-one of the letters, you would have great difficulty reading. Everything in science and math builds on foundational principles, and if you did not learn some of those principles in school, science and math will fail to make sense.

Fortunately, there is a relatively simple solution to this problem. During your daily thirty-minute sessions, start reading easy technical articles that are completely understandable to you. Then slowly challenge yourself. By gradually increasing the complexity of your readings, your knowledge base will grow. This is the same technique that very good teachers utilize for new students who are far behind the other students in a class. (Remember, I was not always at the top of my class. For many years, I was at the bottom.) Today, technological information can be obtained with ease. You can become knowledgeable in almost any area you choose.

Unlike science and math, self-instruction in history and politics requires you to compare and contrast multiple sources to ensure a sound understanding. People love to rewrite history in a way that conforms to their own ideological preferences. It can be instructive to contrast the same event as reported by liberal and conservative observers. It is much easier to formulate informed opinions when you open yourself to different points of view and can draw knowledge from the base you have acquired by reading thirty minutes a day.

It's even important to survey the literature of America's ideological opponents, such as communist and Marxist writers. It is extremely instructive to know what people like community organizer Saul Alinsky thought would be necessary to fundamentally change American society to be acceptable to him. You will be able to decide for yourself whether you agree with this kind of fundamental change, or whether you align with traditional American values. All kinds of belief systems make appearances in current political discourse, so it is important to be able to identify them and to know what you believe about them. Don't just drift and sway along with the rhetoric of skilled political operators who seek to manipulate you.

Religious literature such as the Bible, the Torah, the Koran (Quran), and other texts can shed a great deal of light on certain existing cultures and why there is so much strife associated with the misinterpretation of these books. While researching for his book *Democracy in America* in the 1830s, Alexis de Tocqueville was extraordinarily impressed that American public schools used the Bible to teach morals and values. The Founding Fathers and subsequent generations understood that spirituality was essential to our grounding as political beings, and it is crucial for readers today to familiarize themselves with the part of humanity that is not physical in nature.

Studying world geography and cultures is essential to being well-informed. Just carefully exploring a globe or an atlas will greatly enhance your ability to hold intelligent conversations with a variety of people. It is quite embarrassing that so many Americans have difficulty locating major countries on the globe but have no difficulty following the whereabouts of their favorite celebrity. Not to bash entertainment, but let's use that half an hour per day wisely, because you will surely get a sufficient dose of sports and entertainment news as soon as you turn on the television. Besides, it is a great deal of fun to learn about other cultures and other places.

When I first started serving on corporate boards of directors in the mid-to-late 1990s, I was so unfamiliar with the language of finance that it almost felt like I was in a foreign country. But it is amazing how quickly one can absorb the terms used in business by asking questions and being attentive, as well as by reading financial newspapers and magazines, which are, for the most part, unbiased and full of factual information.

Apparently, relatively few of our elected representatives understand the financial chaos responsible for our national debt, or we would be in better fiscal shape as a nation. If you don't have an understanding of fiscal policies yourself, you won't know if your representative is capable of representing you wisely. So utilize some of your time to learn how to read a financial statement or spreadsheet, and pick a few stocks to follow on the New York Stock Exchange or NASDAQ in order to learn how the vicissitudes of national and international events affect stock prices. You will also discover that your ability to manage your personal finances will increase significantly.

One immediate advantage of your half-hour-per-day reading program will be a dramatic improvement in your ability to spell words correctly. Since you will be looking at words all the time, not only will your spelling consequently improve, but so will your grammar and syntax. Your ability to express yourself orally will be readily noticed by most of your compatriots. You will make much better first impressions, which might result in upward mobility and a variety of new and exciting relationships with successful people. (Remember to remain humble about your rise in status on the way up!)

Many people say that we live in a new educational era where memorized knowledge is not nearly as important as it was in the past, since many people have a smart communication device and can immediately look up virtually any piece of information they need to have. In fact, you may be reading this little book on one right now. However, these devices are much better employed as augmentation for a well-informed individual. It must be remembered that when you hear new information from any source it is immediately evaluated based on what you already know, not what you have access to. In most cases, you are not going to look up whatever you just heard, and the influential effect will be ingrained. The greater your knowledge base, the greater your fortification against unscrupulous attempts at indoctrination.

If you have a normal brain—and if you're reading this book, you probably do—there is no need to bend your political opinions to those of self-proclaimed experts. They will suggest their years of experience in politics make their abilities superior to yours. Years of experience might count if you're flying a jet or performing a complex surgical operation, but gathering and processing information about where to build a school or a bridge depends more on wisdom and the ability to execute a plan well.

Finally, a bonus benefit of reading for thirty minutes a day, in addition to your own transformation into a well-informed and responsible voter, is the tremendous example it sets for the young people in your sphere of influence. The human brain is designed in such a way that youth are much more likely to emulate our actions than to obey our words.

CHAPTER 3

KNOW YOUR NEWS

Without debate, without criticism, no Administration and no country can succeed— and no republic can survive. . . . That is why our press was protected by the First Amendment—the only business in America specifically protected by the Constitution—not primarily to amuse and entertain, not to emphasize the trivial and the sentimental, not to simply "give the public what it wants"—but to inform, to arouse, to reflect, to state our dangers and our opportunities, to indicate our crises and our choices, to lead, mold, educate and sometimes even anger public opinion.

JOHN F. KENNEDY

THOSE WHO DRAFTED our Constitution realized that a press free to tell the truth would be essential to the future's freedom. This is why the First Amendment to the Constitution of the United States ensures freedom of the press. When a government manipulates the press, faith in that government rapidly dissipates.

When the press picks sides in the political arena, it, too, loses the trust of the people. Above all, the press is supposed to truthfully report and meticulously check facts. There should be no tolerance for distortions. When inevitable inaccuracies necessitate corrections, the responsible person should immediately apologize and take corrective actions in plain sight—not in a program footnote or in the back of the paper.

Unfortunately, such distortions tend to occur on a daily basis when the press is biased. When the press favors a specific viewpoint, it gives implicit permission to its advocates to ignore the law and the interests of the people. The side the press favors can assume its malfeasance won't undergo rigorous media scrutiny.

Negative and positive stories about both friends and foes of the press must be reported evenhandedly. If a biased press works in conjunction with dishonest politicians, the populace can be easily deceived into giving up many of their rights and freedoms.

When a major story unfolds and a national news organization totally ignores or barely acknowledges it for ideological reasons, wise consumers should take note and recognize they are very unlikely to get accurate information from that news organization. They should immediately begin looking for more balanced news reporting.

It can be revealing to learn who owns various news outlets and the kind of hiring they do. If the overwhelming majority of an outlet's correspondents are of a particular political persuasion or come from schools of journalism with a particular political slant, evaluate their programming with prudence. If, on the other hand, a national news network has at least a dozen correspondents or contributors of the opposite political spectrum, one can take comfort that they are at least trying to present more than one side of the argument. Since retiring from neurosurgery, I have worked as a contributor for Fox News and have found their promise to be "fair and balanced" an accurate reflection of whom they invite on the air.

When I was growing up, there were only three major national news networks, and they all reported the same stories. Even though some of the anchors were quite ideologically radical, they demonstrated little or no bias in their reporting. Those days are long gone, and political bias is rampant in newsrooms. This means viewers have to invest a bit more effort in obtaining untainted information. The best way to do that is to take in an assortment of news sources when trying to learn about an issue . . . unless you can find one source that goes out of its way to present all the news in a balanced way.

Talk radio is a completely different animal than daily print journalism or network news, because it doesn't even purport to be objective. Programming tends to be rather one-sided with few attempts to accommodate opposing views, however respectful— and in some cases, brilliant—the hosts might be. Talk radio serves as an enjoyable pastime for many, and valuable information can nonetheless be disseminated. It's worth tuning in while driving, exercising, or working, but just to be sure no political agenda slips by you, it's also worth finding out the identities of the station owners and major sponsors.

When it comes to the Internet, it's important to understand that anyone can post anything on the web, which means that people with little or no regard for truthfulness can make their deceptions look legitimate. Be savvy, and cross-reference your Internet research against other sources.

What is at the core of knowing your news sources? Understanding whether the media—acting as the middleman between you and your government—shares your American values summarized in the national Pledge of Allegiance ("One nation under God, indivisible, with liberty and justice for all") and our national statement of values expressed on our money ("Liberty," "*e pluribus unum*," and "In God We Trust").

What do I mean by "American values"?

"One nation" and "e pluribus unum" (Latin meaning "out of many, one")—Our nation was formed out of many independent states and many peoples from different cultures and parts of the world. Our founders expected that all would contribute to a new American culture. It is an exciting and forward-looking vision. Some media embrace it, but others hold America in contempt for not mirroring other nations' cultures more closely. It is important to analyze your news sources to see which category they fit into and whether they correspond with your belief system.

"Under God" and "In God We Trust"—Our nation was formed on a trust in a higher power outside of ourselves. Whenever the people of the United States of America experience a national tragedy, our leaders call upon us to pray to God for strength and comfort. Our Declaration of Independence refers to certain unalienable rights given to us by our Creator. There are many other references to God throughout our judicial and legislative history. With very little investigation, it is quite possible to determine which news sources respect an individual's belief in God and which ones are hostile or condescending to the faithful. The First Amendment guarantees freedom *of* religion, not freedom *from* religion.

"Indivisible"—The founders knew that it would not be easy to hold the grand experiment of the United States together. "Divide and conquer" is an age-old strategy and a very effective technique for destroying enemies. In America today, there are many who fan the flames of division at every opportunity. One of their favorite techniques is pitting blacks against whites and the rich against the poor. They thrive on sorting people into oppressor and victim categories. Media that stoke this kind of divisiveness should be carefully scrutinized. Discerning eyes and ears are necessary to recognize the difference between those who divide with their slick innuendos and those who try to represent all sides of a story.

"Liberty"—The key meaning here is "freedom." I have the greatest respect for those news sources that promote individual freedom to believe or not believe according to the dictates of a person's conscience. Unlike many other nations of the world, America was to be a place where liberty was cherished and no one would be precluded from pursuing those activities that made them happy as long as they did not infringe upon someone else's rights and freedom.

"Justice for all"—The United States of America was founded with an emphasis on the rule of law. The concept of equal justice under the law is such an integral part of our society that we should react with horror any time we see one group or another singled out for persecution or favors from government agencies. Any news organization that consistently ignores such official transgressions is part of the problem. This behavior is exactly the opposite meaning of "liberty and justice for all." News organizations that fail to understand these words are likely to be heavily biased and thus unworthy of voters' trust.

It is very difficult for each one of us to look at ourselves objectively and take stock of our own biases. For this reason, despite the aforementioned revelations, many people will continue to choose their news sources based on their own biases. This is the very reason for the existence of some of these news organizations. It is important for people to recognize that biased news sources can only continue to exist if we continue to patronize them.

CHAPTER 4

RECOGNIZE MANIPULATION

Vote for the man who promises least; he'll be the least disappointing.

BERNARD BARUCH

A LOT OF POLITICIANS want votes by hook or by crook. Their major concern is getting into office and then retaining that office as a permanent job. Originally, people in our country ran for public office in order to serve their fellow citizens. The concept of term limits, therefore, was not a big topic of interest. Most people were quite happy to leave Washington, DC, after they had completed their service.

But in the 1850s congressmen began paying themselves annual salaries. Today, the power and perks bestowed upon Congress are substantial. Before some recently enacted laws restricted the ability of senators and congressmen to benefit from insider information, many of them became multimillionaires during their terms of service. The remaining special treatment and multiple benefits are still enough to attract a large number of people for the wrong reasons. Fortunately there are still many who take very seriously their pledge to represent their constituency's interests.

Honest and decent representatives are very unlikely to engage in voter manipulation. Most of them would prefer to lose an election than to engage in dishonest political trickery. Those with other motives want voters to believe that they have their best interests at heart, and they will say or do almost anything to promote such an image. These people are the manipulators.

One of the manipulators' favorite tactics is giveaways. They work hard to provide all kinds of goodies for their constituents, hoping to ingratiate voters, thereby improving their performance at the polls. Tragically, these politicians run out of other people's money with which to pay for all the promises. This leads to debt accumulated for the next generation. Thomas Jefferson thought this practice was downright immoral, but it has become commonplace today. When the money runs out, so do all the gifts and benefits promised. Think of the panic and civil unrest that ensued a few years ago when Greece was unable to meet its mounting financial obligations to its people.

Another favorite trick of the manipulators is to make ordinary people feel like victims. They can then advocate policies designed to look like they are trying to save the victims and at the same time they can demonize their opponents by trying to convince their constituency that the manipulators' political opponents are the ones who are responsible for their constituency's victimhood.

A classic example of this kind of manipulation is the effort to convince minority voters that anyone advocating officially recognized identification cards is racist, concocting tales of voter fraud. Manipulators will claim that their opponents are trying to suppress the vote by demanding identification cards in areas where they fear they won't do well electorally. I have visited many non-white countries, if you will, in the last few years, and all of them require voter identification before anyone casts a ballot. Surely these nations aren't racist?

In most jurisdictions throughout the United States, it is necessary to present some form of government-issued identification before voting. Although the average American might never even dream of deceitfully voting more than once, there are those who feel that the end justifies the means and will do anything to achieve their goals. I hope everyone (minorities included) across America will take responsibility for having proper identification documents, which are very easy to obtain as long as one does not wait until the last minute to acquire them.

If one lacks the means to pay the fees associated

with official identification documents, he or she can request a fee waiver, and most state governments will oblige. If you have elderly or infirm individuals within your sphere of influence, please make sure they have the appropriate forms of identification, and if they don't, help them to obtain them several months before the election. Then more of us will be able to execute our civic duty as voters.

There would be no need for the predictable cries of racism and discrimination that always surround elections if people would simply plan ahead. I also hope that each will vote their conscience rather than follow the dictates of some party leader who claims to be their savior but does little to improve their circumstances.

Fearmongering is a well-established way to manipulate the emotions of the masses. Fear is such a powerful emotion that it frequently overwhelms rational thought processes. This is the reason why people who are terrified frequently do extremely stupid things. If fear can be cultivated into anger, it is a double win for the manipulators and ensures a very firm grip on their targets. Some of the most effective distortions of the truth are as follows:

"They are taking over our communities and our nation."—Prejudice and racism are bred from ignorance and fear. Political operatives will sometimes try to scare people into believing that members of another race or economic class are going to invade their neighborhood and seize their property. These operatives claim that they can stop the so-called gentrification if elected. Instead of frightening their constituency, politicians ought to offer paths to better community integration, the uniform enforcement of laws, and the protection of private property.

"**Violence is going to continue until the guns are all gone.**"—Blaming gun laws for tragedies instead of human beings is a common ploy of politicians. Everyone in America should understand the significance of the Second Amendment to the Constitution. It gives the citizenry the right to own and bear arms. It is important for citizens to be able to aid the military in the event of a foreign invasion—however unlikely that might seem in the twenty-first century. And just as important, lawful people have the right to defend themselves against individual aggression—or their own corrupt governments. Any politician willing to ignore the Second Amendment to win votes should be regarded with suspicion. (The same goes for any other part of the U.S. Constitution.)

"**They will impose their religion on you.**"— Secular progressives and atheists frequently use this scare tactic to oppose people of faith who are candidates for public office. I am a lifelong member of the Seventh-Day Adventist Church, and I would be the first in line to oppose any attempt to force religion on someone. This nation was started by seekers of religious freedom who were fleeing a state-sponsored church. The politically correct crowd takes this to mean American government should be altogether religion-free. Those who deliberately misinterpret the First Amendment to push their secular agenda should be regarded as dangerous, because if they are willing to trample on the freedom to practice religion publicly, it is very likely they will seek to curtail other freedoms as well.

"They are racists."—Unfortunately, some people readily invoke the "R-word" when any white person opposes a black person's liberal politics. But if a white person opposes a black person's conservative politics, it is another story. Sometimes people do not even recognize their biases until they are pointed out. The truth is, racism exists on both sides of the political aisle, and it must be denounced. As a nation, we have made enormous progress on race over the last half century, and we can be proud of that. But we still have work to do, and we should be vigilant in identifying and exposing this evil in our society wherever it exists. This can only happen if we are unbiased in our assessment of people's speech and actions.

Sadly, voting populations in this country are not immune to the aforementioned manipulation tactics, despite how preposterous they might sound to a rational reader. Recall Marion Barry, the Washington, DC, mayor whom voters returned to office even though FBI footage showed him smoking crack cocaine. And then there is James Michael Curley, the famous Boston mayor who was elected to Boston's aldermen board while serving jail time for a felony conviction. Voters even raised him to the governorship of Massachusetts and then sent him to Congress.

Many people have the feeling that all politicians are corrupt and it really does not matter who they elect to office. This defeatist attitude will destroy our nation if not corrected soon. Voters have an obligation to know the facts about the politicians they are elevating to public office and to choose honorable people over the dishonest. The very best weapon against political manipulation is knowledge. It is extremely difficult to manipulate people who are well equipped with facts. The acquisition of facts requires effort, and each of us has a responsibility to put forth that effort in order to properly exercise the power vested in us by our Constitution.

CHAPTER 5

ASSESS YOUR REPRESENTATIVES

The freedom to criticize judges and other public officials is necessary to a vibrant democracy.
SANDRA DAY O'CONNOR

AMERICANS THINK OF THEIR GOVERNMENT as a democracy. But it is more accurate to classify ours as a democratic republic. The people do not vote their own laws up or down; the representatives they elect do. This is the reason why it is so important to know who your representatives are, how they vote, and how to communicate with them.

We all send representatives to Washington, DC, to vote on federal laws. Similarly, we all send representatives to our respective state capitals to vote on state laws. There are also smaller, although still very important, local councils comprised of elected representatives.

Since readers of this book span many different states, this chapter will focus on the one governmental body we all have in common: the United States Congress, composed of the Senate and the House of Representatives.

Two senators are elected by voters in each state, and you can easily find out who yours are.[1] (See chapter 8 for additional information.)

Depending on how big a state's population is, it might send just one person to the U.S. House of Representatives, as Wyoming does, or as many as fifty-three, in California's case. Using the Internet, you can easily determine who represents you.[2]

Too many Americans feel they have completed their civic responsibilities simply by casting their ballot at the voting booth. But there is more work to be done. Voting merely enables representatives to go to Washington as your advocates. It will be difficult for them to do a good job without input from you, so if you want them to know what you are thinking, call or write a letter. Send them a petition signed by as many of their constituents as you can persuade.

Although your senator or congressman may not take your call or read your letter personally, their staff, paid for by your tax dollars, ought to communicate your message to them and reply courteously to you. Well-informed constituents with high expectations usually get the best results. Remember to keep your questions relevant to current events: the economy, the federal debt, healthcare costs, unemployment, national security, education, etc. Please remember to be respectful of the office. Even if the person representing your state or congressional district is not in your political party or agreeable to you, you must first give respect if you expect respect in return.

Then, consider the substance of your representative's reply. By examining his or her voting history and political funding, you may be able to predict the reply. If you are unsatisfied with the eventual answer you receive, you will need to consider whether your representative is worth your *one vote* in the next election.

What qualifies someone to be your representative in Washington? In a truly democratic spirit, the Founding Fathers did not demand a particular professional background or education, or even literacy, of members of Congress. Voters are free to elect whomever they see fit, as long as the person meets the requirements established in the Constitution: "The Constitution requires that Members of the House be at least 25 years old, have been a U.S. citizen for at least seven years, and live in the state they represent (though not necessarily the same district)."[3] Members of the Senate must be at least thirty years old, have been a U.S. citizen for at least nine years, and live in the state they represent.[4]

Since January 2009, senators and congressmen's base salary has been $174,000, and the minority and majority leaders in both houses receive

$193,400. The Speaker of the House receives $223,500. Members of Congress are also able to earn outside income up to $27,225, unless it is from a place with fiduciary ties to Congress. Some of them teach classes, which an Ethics Committee must first approve.[5]

The perks associated with the office, such as foreign travel expenses, franking privileges, a well-paid staff, and a full pension after five years of service, are numerous. One perk in particular, the Senate Hair Care Shop, has been running yearly deficits in excess of $340,000 since 1997, offering $20 haircuts subsidized by taxpayer dollars.[6] So when Congress votes to cut the budget, this is a place that obviously needs a trim!

Until 1996, members of Congress were wined and dined regularly by lobbyists. That year, a ban on gifts was finally implemented. Now, gifts to congressmen must be valued under $50, and no more than $100 worth of gifts are allowed from any one person or entity in a single year. (Gifts valued at less than $10 do not count toward that limit.) Gifts from foreign entities must be approved by Congress and worth no more than $100. Congressmen and senators are also prohibited from accepting more than $2,600 a year from individuals for campaigns.

It has been said that politicians get elected by promising to go to Washington and drain the swamp. But once they are members of Congress, they discover the swamp feels as good as a hot tub, and they settle right in. What happens when a member of Congress gets too comfortable? Of course, their constituents could vote them out of office in the next election. But if constituents are not knowledgeable about their representatives' behavior, members of Congress can only be removed by resignation, by death, "or by action of the house of Congress in which they are a member by way of an 'expulsion,' or by a finding that in accepting a subsequent 'incompatible' public office, the Member would be deemed to have vacated his congressional seat."[7]

While many slaps on the wrist have been administered to members of Congress, only five in its history have ever been expelled.

Perhaps it is not a coincidence that the congressional gift ban was instituted around the time that the Internet became popular. Checking up on your representative is very easy to do now, thanks to the transparency provided by online media. You can live-stream congressional sessions or read transcripts after a hearing or floor speech. You can learn how various advocacy groups view your representatives and where they fall on the political spectrum compared to other members of Congress.

One of the most important determinations you can make using these online services is whether your representatives have any original thoughts or just follow the herd. If it becomes clear that their political party is more important to them than their country and your values, and if they vote against the wishes of their constituency to support their party without explanation, it may be time to express your displeasure with your *one vote*.

CHAPTER 6

VOTE YOUR VALUES

In selecting men for office, let principle be your guide. Regard not the particular sect or denomination of the candidate—look to his character.

NOAH WEBSTER

IT IS SOMETIMES QUITE SHOCKING when you ask people about their various beliefs and discover that they really have not thought deeply about what is important to them. Without having an understanding of one's own beliefs and values, it is extremely difficult to determine whether a person running for political office shares your beliefs and values. We must each determine what things are most important to us, and we must learn how to prioritize these things when it comes to selecting our representatives.

It is also important to realize that you will never find anyone who agrees with you 100 percent of the time. For some the issue of abortion might be paramount, while for others a candidate's feelings about gun laws might constitute a litmus test. I admire the passion and political commitment required to maintain these positions, but I believe it is a mistake for these so-called "single-issue voters" to ignore all but one of a candidate's stands. In general, it is easier to work with somebody with whom you have only one disagreement than somebody with whom you disagree on virtually everything. This certainly applies when selecting those who will represent us in the federal government.

All major political parties have something known as a party platform. This is a list of the values and beliefs held by that party. Ideally, by looking at a party's platform, voters can decide which party aligns with their value system. Most people do not bother to look at the planks, which are the individual beliefs or values that compose the party's "platform" in this political metaphor. This is particularly true of voters who habitually vote for the same party regardless of the individual candidate's merit. This leads to political stagnation, with offices populated by politicians who grow fat and lazy, feeling little obligation to their constituency. Both the Democratic and Republican Parties in America are very happy about voters who will, out of blind loyalty, vote for them without reading their platforms. The more citizens who lazily vote the party line, the less effort candidates must expend earning votes.

All responsible voters should familiarize themselves with the platform of each major party and deeply reflect on which one fits. Many people are shocked when they discover that their values are more in sync with the party they thought they opposed because political manipulators had done such a splendid job of demonizing the other party with numerous falsehoods. Part of being a knowledgeable voter is familiarizing oneself with both sides of any political argument.

Once you discover and admit to yourself who you really are, the next step is to gather enough courage to actually vote on your convictions rather than on what you think would make you popular and accepted. You don't have any obligation to tell anyone how you voted. Remember, if you compromise your beliefs and vote in a way you believe will allow you to "fit in," you may be compromising your future and that of your children.

A person's belief system is formulated over the course of a lifetime and is based on their life experiences. Those beliefs should not be subjugated to political party affiliation, but rather the people and issues one votes for should be subjugated to their belief system. In other words, party officials should not be telling you how you should vote; rather, you should be telling them how they should act if they want your vote.

One of the issues causing many voters a great deal of consternation is what to do with their religious beliefs when it comes to politics. Separation of church and state does not mean that you must remove your faith from your public life and your voting decisions. Freedom of religion means that you are free to speak about and live according to your faith without threats from the government. *We the people* will decide which are the values and principles that we choose to live by. Each of us must decide for ourselves which of our values and beliefs we are willing to forfeit in order to conform to a political agenda. We must decide which is more important, our faith or politics. We must also decide if we are willing to stand up for our beliefs, or if it is more comfortable to remain silent and avoid controversy. Finally, we must decide if we are going to make decisions based on actual data and historical facts or if we are going to accept the sweet words of ideology and create our own set of facts. The beauty of our system of government is that we get to decide.

CHAPTER 7

SPHERES
OF
INFLUENCE

*An enlightened citizenry is indispensable for the
proper functioning of a republic. Self-government
is not possible unless the citizens are educated
sufficiently to enable them to exercise oversight.*

THOMAS JEFFERSON

THE ORIGINAL VISION FOR AMERICA included a society in which the desires of the people were paramount in the design of policies. People were to be completely free to pursue their dreams and aspirations without interference from neighbors or the government as long as their pursuits did not negatively impact the rights of others. There are others who prefer a different form of government that, instead of placing the people at the pinnacle of power, puts the government in that position and charges the government with the duty of taking care of all the people. Which of these is the best kind of system is a debate that preceded the establishment of America and probably will continue until the end of time. It is, however, very important for voters to understand that if they prefer one of these systems over the other, they have a responsibility to examine the records of people running for public office, hoping to be their representatives, to determine whether those people truly represent them and their preferences.

Is it enough to simply educate yourself about voting, or is it also important to educate those in your sphere of influence? Usually your sphere of influence is much greater than you think. It includes immediate and extended family members, friends, neighbors, work associates, church and club members, and a host of other people you encounter on a regular basis.

Perhaps the most important people in our sphere of influence are our children and grandchildren. Yet we frequently exclude them from serious conversations about the future of America, which is, of course, their future. It is difficult for them to become responsible citizens and well-informed voters if we leave their political education to the school system, which not infrequently has an agenda different from our own.

Have your precious young ones look at objective news programming with you and discuss the content frequently. This will fuel their interest in their schoolwork because you will have provided them with the basis on which they can build their own intelligent opinions. You should also make it your business to know what your children are learning in school. You and other parents certainly can have an influence, but only if you care enough to investigate the curriculum.

Aside from your children and grandchildren, you may have other connections who seek your input on a regular basis, perhaps through Facebook, Twitter, and other forms of social media. Social media is quickly replacing television as the gold standard for reaching thousands or millions of people. Share your insights and opinions with your sphere of influence online, and if you do this in a thoughtful way, you are likely to develop a very substantial following and can wield great influence. However, when talking about others, remember that kindness and respect go a long way toward healing the wounds of division that are eroding our nation. The "my way or the highway" philosophy only works well in a dictatorship. Intelligent people are able to think of more than one way to do things.

The elderly, infirm, and disabled individuals in our society are just as important as everyone else, yet they are frequently forgotten because they are out of sight and thus out of mind. Remember they are in your sphere of influence and, in many cases, they are full of the wisdom that comes with age and are quite willing, even eager, to share their thoughts with a listening ear. Please try to loop into your sphere of influence those who fit this category when it comes to voting. They often care deeply about this country but feel disempowered and will be thrilled with the interest you are giving them. In many cases, their voter registrations have lapsed and you can help to get them restored. Sometimes they are incapable of traveling to a polling place, in which case you can help them obtain an absentee ballot. You could also offer to help them fill it out, particularly if their vision is failing them. Remember to be honest and to not take advantage of them by filling out their ballot according to your wishes rather than theirs. It is time for all of us to reemphasize the importance of integrity and honesty in our lives.

In the whole scheme of things, your *one vote* can decide an election, but broader influences could make the difference between the right candidate winning or losing an election. Americans' pre–Revolutionary War town meetings aired political ideas and values that led to victory in our fight for freedom.

This great country of ours was born of patriotism, not partisanship. It is only if we are willing to vote according to our values and not according to party dictates that we will be able to achieve a truly free and prosperous society that works for everyone and not just the politically astute.

CHAPTER 8

PRACTICAL STEPS

Democracy cannot succeed unless those who express their choice are prepared to choose wisely. The real safeguard of democracy, therefore, is education.

FRANKLIN D. ROOSEVELT

WHEN THE FOUNDERS ESTABLISHED the Constitution of the United States (http://archives.gov/exhibits/charters/constitution.html), it took days for news to travel across what at the time were thirteen states running up and down the Eastern Seaboard. In fact, the first daily newspaper was not printed until 1784. Today, we cannot imagine living without the Internet, where information is not only abundant but often available in real time.

As part of our effort in writing this book, and in an attempt to provide readers with as much practical assistance as possible to help them become more informed voters, we explored the Internet to find what we believe to be nonpartisan and unbiased sources of information readily available to the voting public. On the following pages, we have provided URLs to some sites where the people involved seem to be committed to providing accurate and nonpartisan information for those who want to be more informed as citizens.

The Internet expands and contracts almost daily

with new sites coming online and existing sites either going away or becoming obsolete. Because of this dynamic and constant change, and in order to provide a location for you to easily find the information, we have also commissioned a website, OneVoteBook.com, to be a central launching point to these sites. As new, meaningful, and useful sites are discovered or existing sites go away or stagnate, we will make our best efforts to keep this simple site updated.

Seeking information often starts with finding an answer to a simple question, and more often than not, that answer presents a new question or set of questions. As you read this final chapter, we challenge you to use these sites, or others you might find, to answer these questions:

1. How do my values line up with those of my political party?
2. Who is my senator and/or congressman, and if I ask him/her a question in an e-mail, what kind of response will I get?
3. What kind of answer to my question should I expect back from my representative?

Party Affiliation

ISideWith.com has an interesting political quiz (http://ISideWith.com/political-quiz) that walks you through a series of questions. You can answer each question with a yes or no, but if you feel your response cannot be answered with a simple yes or no, they provide expanded options to choose from. They also allow you to prioritize every question on a five-point scale from least important to most important.

After answering all the questions and selecting "Show My Results," you will be presented with feedback showing how your views and values coincide with various political parties.

Know Your Representatives

Both the United States Senate (www.senate.gov) and the House of Representatives (www.house.gov) have websites with a wealth of information, especially when it comes to daily activities. But one of the best features of both sites is a way to find and contact your senator (http://goo.gl/k813) or congressman/congresswoman (http://goo.gl/nml4N). You should never be afraid to contact your representatives. After all, they work for you, and your taxes pay a portion of their salaries.

A Representative's Legislative Record

GovTrack.us is an impressive site. The depth and breadth of its information and objective is something all the contributors to the site should be very proud of. As it says on the "About" page, "The site helps ordinary citizens find and track bills in the U.S. Congress and understand their representatives' legislative record."[1]

In the past, knowing your representative's legislative record took place during an election campaign; the sitting candidate would tell you his or her version, and the candidate's opponent would tell you his or her own version. Typical of two opposing points, the truth was somewhere in the middle. GovTrack .us takes the self-serving factor out of the equation and provides a straightforward and factual analysis of every representative. By clicking on "Browse" and then "Members of Congress" (https://govtrack.us /congress/members) on the GovTrack.us website, you can enter your home address and find your Senator and House representatives. When you click on the representative you want more information on, you will see a profile of the person, showing:

- **Sponsorship Analysis**—A chart showing how the representative compares to other representatives based on a leadership and ideology scoring system.
- **Committee Membership**—Committees the representative is a member of.
- **Bills Sponsored**—List of bills sponsored by the representative.
- **Voting Record**—Text and graph showing

how often the representative was present and voted.

Because of the wealth of data that GovTrack.us captures, it can be difficult and time-consuming to process all the details, which is why they provide a "Report Card" on every representative's profile page. When you go to the representative's report card, you will get a consolidated view of how your representative is working for you and how they compare to other representatives.

Know Your Candidates

Project Vote Smart (votesmart.org) is another impressive website with a wealth of information that covers both national and state elections, including any referendums or initiatives on the ballots, but it is one of their tools that impressed me the most. Their VoteEasy (http://VoteSmart.org/voteeasy) animated app gives you a chance to see how your views compare to candidates in an election. By choosing issues listed along the top of the page, you can gain an understanding through a variety of topics on how your views compare to the candidates vying for your vote. As you select your opinion on a particular topic, you will see candidates move either forward (view similar to yours) or backward (view dissimilar to yours).

Political Funding

It is no secret that it takes money to win an election, but how much of and where a candidate's money comes from should be known and available in one location. OpenSecrets.org provides a consolidated fundraising report on every candidate. When on their site, go to "Politicians & Elections"/"Congressional Elections" (http://OpenSecrets.org/races) and discover where and how much money is coming in for your candidate and the opposing candidate.

Voter Eligibility and Registration

To be eligible to vote in the United States, you must first be a U.S. citizen. Most states require you to be at least eighteen years of age, but in some states you can vote as early as seventeen. However, you cannot vote if you are not registered. Voter registration is usually required in advance of election day. For most states, you must register about thirty days before the election, but this varies from state to state. Some states even allow you to register online, but most states require registration to be completed in person or by mail. Check to see what the lead time is in your state at http://www.usa.gov/Citizen/Topics/Voting/Register.shtml. The USA.gov site has information about how to register (http://USA.gov/Citizen/Topics/Voting.shtml), and in most states you can register by mail to vote using the National Mail

Voter Registration Form (http://www.eac.gov/voter _resources/register_to_vote.aspx), doing it all from the comfort of your own home.

Methods of voting vary from state to state and other local jurisdictions as well. However, the majority of states allow for early voting by mail, and voters who may not be able to cast their vote in person can do so in advance of election day by absentee ballot. For more information on elections and voting, go to http://www.usa.gov/Citizen/Topics /Voting/Learn.shtml.

It should be noted that according to your state of residence, you could be eligible to take time off from work to vote. Check this website to find the laws that are applicable in your state: http://www .workplacefairness.org/votingrights.

The Americans with Disabilities Act of 1991 has improved the quality of life for those with disabilities in substantive ways. One of them is access on voting day. For more information, visit http://www .eac.gov/voter_resources/resources_for_voters_with _disabilities.aspx.

Civics Refresher

Back in the 1970s, we had Schoolhouse Rock's "I'm Just a Bill" (http://youtu.be/tyeJ55o3El0). Today, learning civics is interactive thanks to iCivics (http:// iCivics.org). iCivics is founded and led by retired

Associate Justice of the United States Supreme Court Sandra Day O'Connor. The site offers tools that help students, both young and old, learn about our system of government through games that place students in different civic roles and give them agency to address real-world problems and issues.

A CALL TO ACTION

IF YOU HAVE READ THIS ENTIRE BOOK, you are obviously a person who desires to become a more informed voter. Congratulations, and thank you for your commitment to excellence as a citizen of the greatest nation in history. If we each understand and constantly remind ourselves that voting is the principal way we can and will control our government, we can make certain that government is a reflection of **all** the people and that *it* works for *us* and not vice versa.

The Internet continues to change how people do business, get an education, and socialize. Some of these changes have been good and some not so good, but what we do know is that the Internet has empowered you to be more informed and to be directly involved with what happens in the democratic process guaranteed by our Constitution. It's up to you to take the first step and seek answers to your questions, and then you must vote your convictions and hold your representatives accountable for their exercise of the power bestowed on them by voters. It is our hope that this book will help you realize that you can work with the Internet to make yourself a more informed voter, even if you have never had success on the Internet before.

We trust that this book has been a blessing to you and will truly assist you in becoming a more informed voter. Please retain it as a resource for the months and years ahead, regardless of your political persuasion.

Our ultimate goal for *One Vote* is that it will help to raise up an Army of Believers made up of people who have determined that their vote counts and that they can make their voice heard through their vote. It will be an Army of Believers who understand that they can actually make a difference with their vote. They will have determined that they can and will know what they believe about what is good for America, will inform themselves as to which candidate on their ballots comes closest to those beliefs, and will then go and vote based on their values. Our hope is that this will be an Army of Believers who enlist into that Army their family members and their friends, encouraging them to become active citizens of our great ***one nation,*** *under God, indivisible, with liberty and justice for all.* Then, one voter and *one vote* at a time, we can hold our elected leaders accountable to the voice of the American people.

One last thought from Thomas Jefferson:

> I know no safe depository of the ultimate powers of the society, but the people themselves: and if we think them not enlightened enough to exercise their control with a wholesome discretion, the remedy is not to take it from them, but to inform their discretion by education.[1]

OneVoteBook.com

This title is also available in an e-book version on Bookshout.com.

HAVE YOU READ DR. CARSON'S
#1 *NEW YORK TIMES* BESTSELLER
ONE NATION?

If not, here's a free sample of
chapter 1 to get you started.

SAVING OUR
FUTURE

*Godliness exalts a nation, but sin is a disgrace to any
people.*

PROVERBS 14:34

SEVERAL YEARS AGO I took a trip to Alaska, and my hosts offered to send me on an excursion in their private plane to see the glaciers in the area. I was extremely excited and eagerly accepted the offer. I was less excited when I saw the single-engine prop plane that would be used by the pilot. He assured me that he had flown this mission many times and that the plane was very safe, so we headed out.

As the plane took off, I marveled at the beautiful scenery. As we flew over the mountaintop and dropped into the valley, it almost seemed as if we were on another planet. The glaciers were awe inspiring and I quietly thanked God for the opportunity to view these natural wonders.

As I was enjoying the sights, heavy cloud cover descended on the valley severely obscuring our view. The small plane was not equipped for instrument-only flight, so the pilot announced that we were going to climb through the clouds as rapidly as we could without going into a stall, and that we should clear the mountaintops that surrounded us. He spoke calmly, but I could detect the uncertainty in his voice. Deeply concerned, I entered into prayer and reminded myself that God is in charge even when we are in grave danger.

After several intense minutes of upward flight, there was a break in the clouds and we cleared the mountain peaks by just a few feet. Relieved, I thanked the pilot for his quick and decisive action that saved our lives. I was never so happy to be on the ground as when we landed at the small airstrip.

Our nation is in trouble today, and our only chance is to take quick and decisive action the way the pilot did in Alaska. Shrugging and hoping that something good would happen was not a viable choice for us as our plane hurtled toward the mountain, and it is not a wise choice for us today. Doing everything we could while beseeching the mercies of God paid big dividends in the Alaskan sky, and prayerful action could make all the difference in the problems America faces now.

Many Americans argue that our nation's future does not need to be saved and that we are in very good shape. They think that only partisans are skeptical about our future and that people say negative things in order to make the current administration look bad. They see the beautiful view that is America, but they don't have the common sense and wisdom to look for the lowering clouds that obscure the mountains.

It is true that we are enjoying the benefits of the system set up by our founders, and we are relatively quite comfortable because previous generations have made good choices. Nevertheless, the fog has been gathering for years, and we must act quickly and decisively to deal with substantial issues if we don't want to destroy our children's future.

A quick glance at a newspaper should be enough to perceive the warning signs. As far as education is concerned, we have made a lot of progress in being politically correct, but very little progress in basic education, particularly in areas like math and science. The secular progressive movement completely denies any moral backsliding and feels that we have made substantial progress as a nation with respect to great moral issues like abortion, gay marriage, and helping the poor, but in reality we are losing our moral compass and are caught up in elitism and bigotry. On top of that, our national debt and the passage of Obamacare are threatening the financial future of our nation. Worst of all, we seem to have lost our ability to discuss important issues respectfully and courteously and cannot come together enough to begin to solve our problems.

We each need to take an active role in changing

the course of our nation if we are to live up to the motto "one nation under God, indivisible, with liberty and justice for all." We are the pinnacle nation in the world right now, but if the examples of Egypt, Greece, Rome, and Great Britain teach us anything, it is that pinnacle nations are not guaranteed their place forever. If we fail to rediscover the basic principles of common sense, manners, and morality, we will go the same way they did. Fortunately, our downward pathway is not an inexorable one. It is not too late to learn from the mistakes of those who preceded us and take the kinds of corrective action that will ensure a promising future for those who come after us.

Communities, political parties, business organizations, the news media, educational institutions, and the government can all work to turn our nation around, but the most important changes will be made by you and me, the American individuals. Each of us can control only our own behavior, but if we all take action individually, our actions will collectively have a significant impact on the direction of our nation. As individuals, we can educate ourselves and our children, cultivate the art of compromise, pray for wisdom, and hold our representatives accountable. Each of us can positively affect our nation just by making ourselves (and those in our spheres of influence) aware of the fact that we are being used as pawns by those who try to tell us what we should think as opposed to using our own common sense.

As an example of cloudy thinking that threatens common sense, consider the recent furor over voter ID cards. I travel to many nations of the world, and recently I've taken it upon myself to ask citizens of those other countries how they prevent voter fraud. I have yet to find a nation that does not require some type of official voter identification card or mechanism to ensure that the voter is who they say they are. This is basic common sense, yet some members of our society who have co-opted the media have convinced ordinary Americans that there is some type of discrimination going on when we require the same thing of those voting in our country. This would not even be an issue if political groups weren't trying to curry favor with certain groups of voters. Instead of being whipped into a frenzy over a nonissue, it is my hope and prayer that individual Americans will educate themselves on this issue, seek to understand one another's values, allow common sense to prevail, and reject those who try to politicize almost everything to their own advantage.

When I was a child, there was a common saying: "Sticks and stones may break my bones but names will never hurt me." I'm not sure that children today have ever heard that expression and certainly the adults don't seem to know it any longer. Special interest groups tell our country's citizens that they should be easily offended by simple words or suggestions. By taking umbrage so readily, people shift the discussion from the subject matter to the person making the comment, which is a desirable thing to do only if you don't have a good argument. This is also a good way to keep people at one another's throats constantly so they can't form a united front and deal logically with the many real issues facing the nation. Individually, Americans need to choose to be the bigger person, overlook offense, and be willing to have candid discussions about volatile issues.

There have been many stories recently about the bullying epidemic that seems to be occurring in our public school system. We should not be terribly surprised by this because children emulate what they see adults doing. One does not have to look at television for very long or listen to the radio for an extended period before one sees supposedly rational and mature adults vehemently attacking one another, calling each other names and acting like third graders. I have grown used to dealing with people who resort to name-calling at the drop of a hat by saying, "Now that you have had an opportunity to engage in a gratuitous attack, is it possible for us to return to the subject matter at hand?" I refuse to engage in the grade-schoolyard tactics of name-calling and mean-spirited comments when we have so many important issues to solve. We can help our nation quite a bit if we refrain from getting into our respective corners and throwing hand grenades at each other, and instead try to understand the other's viewpoint, reject the stifling of political correctness, and engage in intelligent civil discussion.

A suitably thick skin, common sense, and manners are of limited use without education. I'm always fascinated by some of the "man on the street" episodes on *The Tonight Show with Jay Leno* or *Watters' World* on Fox, where Jay or Jesse asks people for very basic information regarding the significance of a particular day or some historical event and many of them have no clue about the right answer. Our nation's founders felt very strongly that our system of government could only survive with a well-informed and educated populace. They understood that if the populace reached the point of not being able to critically analyze information, it would easily fall prey to slick politicians and unethical news media. All citizens need to arm themselves with a basic knowledge of American history and stay abreast of current events, analyzing them with respect to history. Knowledge is power and at a time when the people are becoming increasingly impotent while the government grows larger and more powerful, it is vital that we arm ourselves with knowledge.

Finally, each of us must have courage. I have encountered countless thousands of Americans, as I've traveled around the country recently giving speeches, who resonate very strongly with the concepts that I'm putting forward but who have been beaten down. They have mistaken the false unity of political correctness and submission for the true unity that comes with liberty, justice, and responsibility. This unity doesn't succeed without some conflict, but it is far healthier than silence and is worth the fight. I've been spreading the word that we must have enough backbone to stand up to the secular progressives who insist on fundamentally changing America into something that we would not recognize as our hard-won government of, by, and for the people. Because there are consequences for standing up for your beliefs in the current distorted version of America, one has to be very courageous when standing up to malicious influences or even while engaging in healthy dialogue with our neighbors about important issues.

The bottom line is that our country is in the process of undergoing fundamental radical changes while rapidly moving away from the "can-do" attitude that made us the most prosperous and beneficent superpower the world has ever known. If each of us sits back and expects someone to take action, it will soon be too late. But as of today, it is still not too late to join the battle to save our nation and pass on to our children and grandchildren something we can all be proud of.

OTHER BOOKS BY
BEN CARSON, MD

One Nation: What We Can All Do to Save America's Future, 2014

America the Beautiful: Rediscovering What Made This Nation Great, 2012

Take the Risk: Learning to Identify, Choose, and Live with Acceptable Risk, 2007

The Big Picture: Getting Perspective on What's Really Important in Life, 1999

Think Big: Unleashing Your Potential for Excellence, 1992

Gifted Hands: The Ben Carson Story, 1990

NOTES

Due to the length and complexity of some of the links in these notes, Google's URL shortener service (http://goo.gl) has been used to shorten all links to make them easier to share.

PREFACE
1. "2012 Voter Turnout," Bipartisan Policy Center, November 8, 2012, http://goo.gl/L7NsOc.

CHAPTER 1: YOU ARE THE PINNACLE OF POWER
1. *The Founders Constitution*, Amendment I, Thomas Jefferson to Edward Carrington, http://goo.gl/Q6bBjZ.
2. See Matthew 12:25; http://goo.gl/ldEOBz.

CHAPTER 5: ASSESS YOUR REPRESENTATIVES
1. See the Senate's website to find out who your senators are: http://goo.gl/k813. There is more information available in chapter 8.
2. See the House of Representatives' website to find out who your representative is: http://goo.gl/K7VYX.
3. "Constitutional Qualifications," United States House of Representatives, http://goo.gl/mYavwV.
4. "Constitutional Qualifications for Senator," United States Senate, http://goo.gl/gZuGHS.
5. Ida A. Brudnick, *Congressional Salaries and Allowances* (Washington, DC: Congressional Research Service, 2014). You can read the report at http://goo.gl/xMyhe (PDF).

6. Lynn Hulsey, "Senate Even Losing Money on Haircuts," *Dayton Daily News*, February 9, 2013, http://goo.gl/OOhQ3Z.

7. Jack Maskell, *Recall of Legislators and the Removal of Members of Congress from Office* (Washington, DC: Congressional Research Service, 2012), 2. See http://goo.gl/rnWgOF (PDF).

CHAPTER 8: PRACTICAL STEPS

1. "About GovTrack.us," GovTrack.us, http://goo.gl/hd9Hyz.

A CALL TO ACTION

1. Thomas Jefferson, Letter to William Charles Jarvis, September 28, 1820, http://goo.gl/EXQs5P.

Having purchased a copy of
One Vote: Make Your Voice Heard,
you are entitled for a limited time
to a free e-book edition.
To redeem your copy, please go to
http://bookshout.com/onetyndale.